# Southampton Castle

John Hodgson

SOUTHAMPTON CITY MUSEUMS ARCHAEOLOGY SERIES

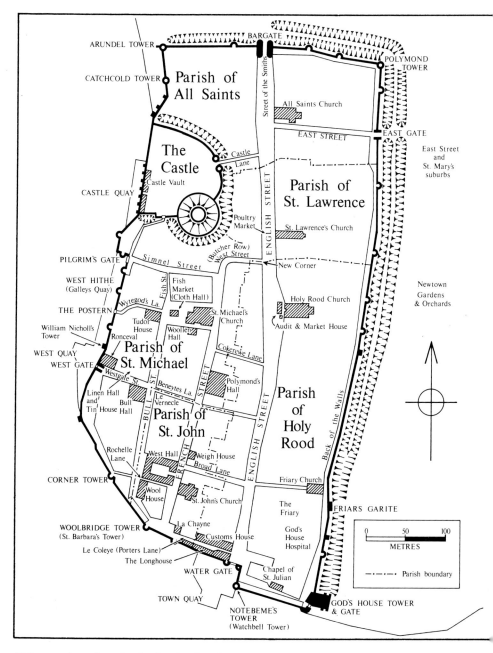

*This map shows how the Castle related to the rest of Medieval Southampton.*

*In spite of redevelopment and the building of some new roads, this pattern of streets can still be followed today. Many of the street names have remained unaltered, and landmarks such as the Bargate, God's House Tower and the town's West Wall still stand.*

2

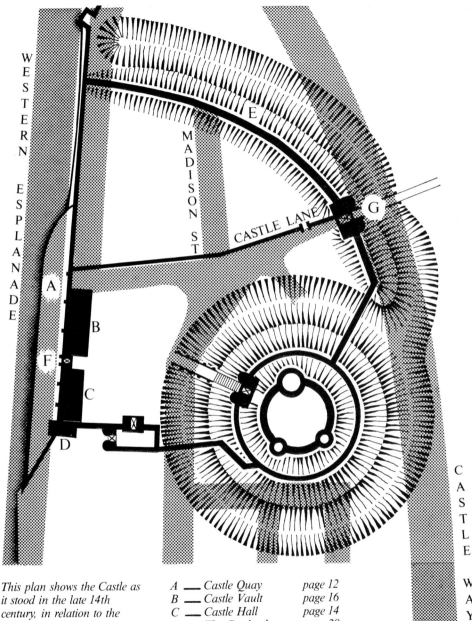

This plan shows the Castle as it stood in the late 14th century, in relation to the modern roads which are shaded in grey. A great deal of this structure, and all of its banks and ditches, has now disappeared, but the various remains are referred to in this booklet.

# INTRODUCTION

A medieval ship's captain, putting in to the busy quays beneath Southampton's walls in the year 1400, would have seen a very different city from that which now stands. At that time, much of what is now the western dockland was still navigable water, and the sea washed against the footings of the town's southern and western walls.

High above these walls towered the keep of Southampton Castle, a prominent landmark for many miles – in fact, it once served as a mark for shipping, with a brazier at its highest point to act as a lighthouse at night. In 1400 the Castle was at its strongest; recently rebuilt, and the key to the defences of one of England's richest and most important sea-ports.

Yet only fragments of this important building still exist. Over five hundred years have passed since changes in military strategy made the Castle obsolete, even as its final rebuilding was completed. Weathering, neglect, and demolition for building stone have completely destroyed the great keep; the curtain walls to the south, east and much of the north are gone; the deep defensive ditches are silted-up and built over, and even the great mound on which the keep was built has largely disappeared. All

that remains above ground are the foundations of the North Wall, the West Wall, and a part of the Castle Hall and Vault.

So to understand Southampton Castle it is necessary to reconstruct it on paper, using the evidence provided by the documents of the time, and the archaeologists' evidence from their excavations on the site. Both of these methods have drawbacks. Documents may be incomplete, sometimes contradictory or not very clear in their meaning. Also, although an account for repairs may show us what work was intended, it cannot tell us how much work the contractor actually carried out. Archaeology can give us more concrete evidence, but unfortunately only a small fraction (10%) of the Castle site has been available for excavation and that fraction has not been in those areas where much useful information might be expected.

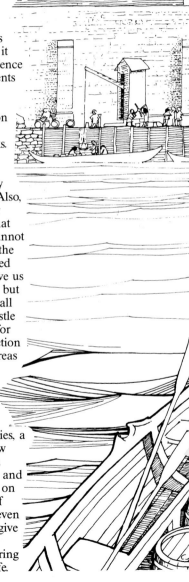

Despite these difficulties, a great many facts are now known about the Castle. Many more are needed, and the theories constructed on the available facts are of course incomplete, but even so it is now possible to give a broad picture of Southampton Castle during its 300 years of useful life.

*French wine-casks being unloaded off Castle Quay.*

# THE NORMAN CONQUEST

In 1066, Duke William of Normandy landed with his followers in England. By the end of the close-fought battle of Hastings, the last of the Saxon kings was dead and Duke William able to become William I of England.

That is, William was in theory able to become King. To be ruler of the country in practical terms meant far more work than merely winning one battle. The Normans were not popular rulers; they were a fairly small, armed expeditionary force in a well-populated and hostile country.

This was the first and most urgent reason behind the Normans' massive programme of castle-building: to provide the new rulers and their troops with secure bases against the possibility of rebellion. These huge, forbidding structures were impossible to storm or capture without a well-disciplined and equipped force. Equally important was their psychological effect; the castles enhanced the status and authority of their builders, and clearly stated the Norman's intention to stay in England and to rule it on their own terms.

There were other reasons. Well-defended strongholds were needed at strategic points to protect the country from further invasion; having gained his kingdom, William did not want anyone else to copy him. There was no banking system as we know it. Wealthy men needed safe walls to protect their cash reserves, and similarly the royal mints and valuable cargoes needed protection. And as time went on, many lords engaged in castle-building as a way of emphasising their own status and importance.

This process naturally took many years to reach completion. The first strongholds of the Normans, raised under the threat of sudden rebellion in the years following the Conquest, were generally built of timber for speed of construction. But later, as the reorganized state found its feet, and as time, money, and labour became available, the timber was replaced with solid masonry.

# THE CASTLE'S ORIGINS

It is not known exactly when the first phase of the Castle was built. Before the Normans came there was already a thriving Saxon town at Southampton and it contained a Royal Burgh or fortification, but the Normans chose a different site for their castle, to the north of the Burgh. The earliest written evidence for a Norman structure occurs in 1153, but even this refers to a "fortified residence" rather than a "castle" as such.

However, Southampton was such an important site – both as a trading centre, and as a possible target for raiders or invasion forces – that it seems unlikely that two such experienced soldiers as William I and his co-regent, William FitzOsbern, would have simply overlooked it. It is even more unlikely in that FitzOsbern was based in Hampshire, and is known to have been an enthusiastic castle-builder. There are two other fragments of evidence which may imply a founding-date of between 1066 and 1100. One is the discovery of two William I coins on the site. The other is the size of the Castle motte, the huge artificial mound on which the Castle Keep was built. This is comparable in size with those of other castles of an early date; later mottes were smaller.

Southampton stands upon fairly level ground, and there were no naturally strong positions on which to build the Castle. The best that could be done was to choose a site in the north-west of the peninsula, where the sea, and a low gravel cliff rising from the shoreline, helped

its western defences. Apart from this, the evidence for the rest of the Castle's structure is fragmentary, and much has to be conjectured. The plan can only show a reasonable interpretation of what evidence exists for the Castle in the early 12th century.

*This tower-block stands on the site of the Castle Keep. Although the motte is much reduced, the photograph shows the steep rise from the old shore level.*

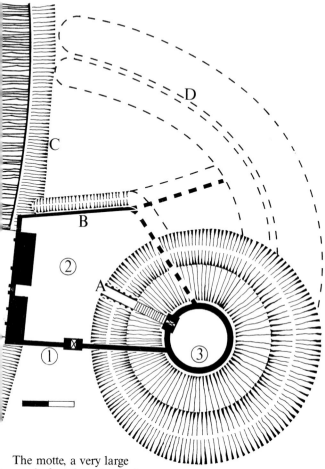

All of the Norman "motte and bailey" castles had three main components:

1 The CURTAIN WALLS, which formed the main perimeter defence against attacks.

2 The BAILEY, a protected enclosure which could contain the local population and livestock in times of conflict.

3 The KEEP, which was usually elevated on a mound (the Motte), acted as a look-out post, firing platform, and second line of defence if the curtain walls were breached or the gates forced.

The motte, a very large mound of earth and gravel, was certainly raised at this time and was surrounded by a deep ditch, 20m wide where it ran outside the Castle walls. At the top of the motte a shell keep was erected; this was a ring of walling, with buildings backing-on to the wall inside it. Access from the keep to the bailey was probably via a wooden bridge across the interior ditch (A).

The exact course of the curtain walls, and therefore the size and number of baileys, is uncertain. The south wall with its gate has been established; to the west the outside walls of Castle Hall and Castle Vault form part of the perimeter, but to the North there are two possible interpretations.

A wall and ditch (B) have been found, which may have been the boundary of

the defences at this stage. This would give a single, fairly small bailey. However, this wall and ditch may have only divided the inner from an outer bailey. The outer bailey would have been bounded by the gravel cliff (C) and the northern rampart and ditch (D). This rampart and ditch cannot yet be reliably dated, and the question must remain open.

# THE EFFECTS OF TRADE

The Castle owed its origins to military necessity, but it was trade which gave the impetus for its upkeep and enlargement during the next two centuries.

England's trade during the early medieval period was on the increase. Exports of raw wool – the basis of much of the country's wealth – were being made to the Baltic countries, to France and Spain. Imports of many luxury goods, especially wine, were coming into England, and Southampton – with a good,

sheltered harbour on the South coast, and dry tracks along chalk ridge country to link it with London and the rest of the country – was ideally situated as a trading port and distribution centre.

This largely accounts for the monarchy's interest in Southampton, quite apart from the fact that it was a Royal castle. The wine trade was of great importance to the King as a source of revenue, from the levies imposed by his representatives on imports. In addition, the King

himself imported a great deal of wine; his position, status and popularity demanded that he entertain a considerable number of people, on a lavish scale, all the year round.

Therefore the main focus of royal concern and expenditure at Southampton Castle was not so much on the defences as on the main economically useful structures – the quay and the two strong warehouses, Castle Hall and Castle Vault.

*The wide extent of Southampton's trade is confirmed by archaeological evidence. Jugs found in Southampton from Saintonge (left) and Normandy (right).*

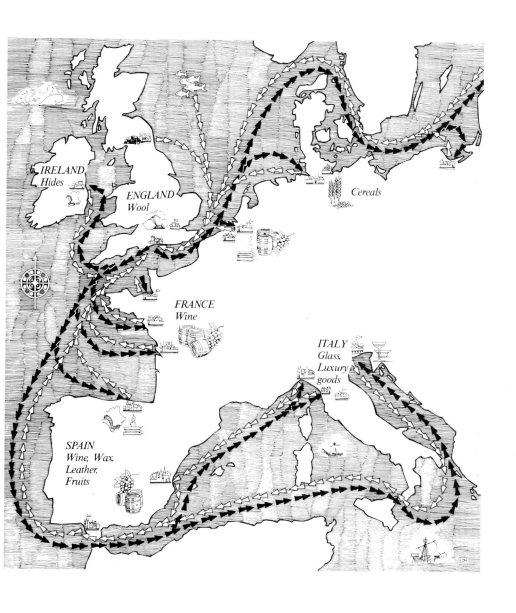

*This map shows the extent and variety of the goods which were traded by Southampton's merchants all over Europe.*

11

# CASTLE QUAY

Castle Quay has never been excavated, and the stretch of tidal water in which it stood is now dry land, covered by a busy tarmac road. Even its exact dimensions are uncertain; all that we know about it comes from documentary evidence. From its first mention in 1189 there are frequent references to expenditure for repairs and maintenance, which shows its economic importance – and, probably, heavy usage. It seems likely that the quay was not all one structure, but was built partly of timber with other sections of stonework. Even at that time the tidal waters alongside the quay would not have been very deep, and this problem may have been made worse by the Castle occupants' habit of throwing their refuse into the water (the absence of refuse deposits elsewhere suggests that this is how they disposed of it!). Trading ships would have lain to anchor in the deeper water of the river channel, and cargoes ferried to and from them in lighters.

*Until the early years of this century, tidal water reached almost to the foot of the Castle walls.*

*(Reproduced by permission of the Southampton City Archives Dept.)*

*Now that the land has been reclaimed, tarmac covers whatever is left of the Castle Quay. The dotted line shows its probable extent.*

Castle Hall is the largest of the Castle's buildings that still remains, and the recently installed stairways and catwalks make it possible to examine the building in detail.

Castle Hall has passed through several stages of use and construction. Initially it was built at some time between 1100 - 1150 as a "first-floor hall house"[1]. This was a typical design of the period in which the whole of the first floor was taken up by a large dwelling-hall. This upper floor is now gone, but the square recesses which held the floor timbers can still be seen in the east wall.

The ground floor of this building was used for storage, probably of the King's casks of French wine. There were at least two doorways (now blocked up) in the West wall, which would have given access to the Castle Quay; in the south-west corner are the remnants of the stone spiral staircase which connected the two floors of the Hall.

Castle Hall was considerably altered in the early 13th century, when the timber floor of the first storey hall was removed and a stone barrel vault inserted in its place[2]. Parts of this vaulting can be seen projecting from the walls, and some sections have been restored. The exact purposes for which the building was redesigned are

uncertain, but it may well
have served on occasions as
a law court for Royal
officials, the "justices-in-eye".

Before leaving the Hall, it
is interesting to notice the
two gunports in the West
wall. These were originally
inserted about 1380,
although their present form
on the inside of the wall is a
much later remodelling.
They have an important
bearing on the later history
of the Castle.

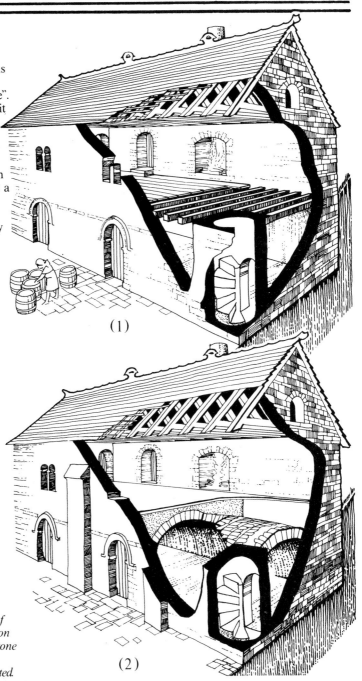

(1)

*Castle Hall from its north-
western corner. The square
holes for the floor timbers of
the first phase can be seen on
the east wall. Parts of the stone
barrel-vault of the second
phase have been reconstructed.*

(2)

# CASTLE VAULT

Castle Vault was probably constructed about 1193, not long before the barrel vault was added to Castle Hall. The construction principle was similar, and the result a very impressive structure – the only part of the Castle buildings to have stayed intact up to the present day. Castle Vault also had an upper storey, although none of this remains; the Vault itself served the same purpose as that in Castle Hall – secure storage for the King's wines.

There was only one entrance to the vault from the quay, but a small window gives additional lighting at the end furthest from the doorway. The vaulted roof is supported by eight ribs; the ribs in turn once rested on sixteen corbels, but only four now remain relatively intact. They have carved decorations typical of this period.

We have seen part of the Castle's role as a military stronghold, and the way that trade affected its development. A third factor was its function as a royal castle.

A medieval king was rarely found in one place for very long. There were several reasons for this; his roles of head of state, military commander, and principal magistrate of the realm all demanded his actual presence. The threat of a coup d'etat by one of the King's more ambitious nobles was never entirely absent, and the King needed to keep in close touch with the country to maintain his authority and control. He had to maintain personal leadership of his armed force, and to carry out his administrative and legal functions a secondary army of officials, clerks and general servants had to move with him. This, then, was the Kings' court; and wherever it went it had to be fed, entertained and housed. This was another reason why moves were so frequent and hunting so popular, for no one area could afford the expense of feeding the Court for very long.

The Royal Castles served as "hotels" for the King and his retinue, and it is natural that various works aimed at improving the quality of life within Southampton Castle were made at this time.

There was considerable expenditure during the 13th century, some of which was on the defensive works and waterfront, but much on the domestic aspect of the buildings. The chapel of St. Nicholas (no longer standing, but believed to have been on the site of the Juniper Berry public house) was re-roofed in 1253, and a few years later new vestments and church furnishings were bought for this "King's Chapel". Earlier in the century payments were made for improvements to the King's houses and chambers at Southampton Castle and, as we have seen, Castle Hall was remodelled with a stone vault. The sanitary facilities of the Castle also received attention; this was ordered by Henry III – a monarch known for his interest in the proper maintenance of his Royal privies. In this instance the documentary evidence is confirmed by archaeology, as is shown below (p.20).

# THE GARDEROBE

In 1252, an order was made for a "new Warderobe for the Queen". This was in fact a garderobe or privy block, and it was constructed as a rectangular tower at the south-west corner of the Castle. The tower has long since been demolished, but the garderobe among its foundations has been excavated and can now be seen.

This long chamber, which is the cess-pit of the privy, is unique for secular architecture of this period. Similar types are known for monastic sites, where "reredorters" were sometimes built over streams or culverts, but the Southampton Castle garderobe was both better made and probably more efficient. The walls are of very finely dressed and close-fitting stone, as are the flagstones of the floor, which must have greatly helped in flushing it clean. This happened automatically; the arched entrance at the far end connected, via a tunnel through the tower wall, to the sea. Thus the rising and falling of the tides regularly flushed it out.

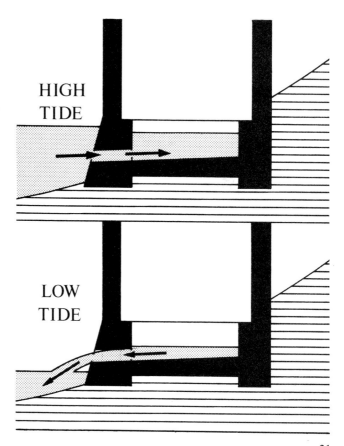

HIGH TIDE

LOW TIDE

*This photograph shows the fine craftsmanship of the masons, who dressed and fitted the stonework to a smooth finish – easily flushed clean by the tide.*

Despite other expenses, the Castle defences were not entirely neglected during this time. However, there seems to be a shift of emphasis away from the motte and keep of the Castle, in favour of its perimter defences – the ramparts and walling which surrounded the bailey. An inquiry into the state of the Castle was made in 1260, and in 1282 and 1286 "Murage Grants" were made to raise the money for repairs. These were, in effect, tolls levied at the city gates on goods entering or leaving the city.

The building works of 1240-1286 improved the Castle considerably, and it began to take its definitive form.

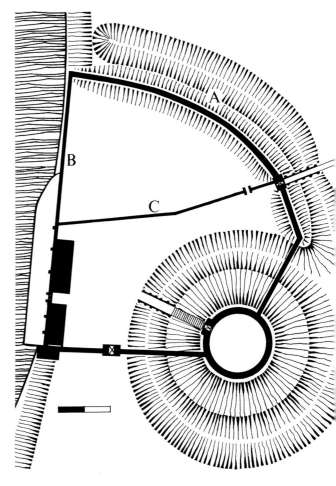

The northern rampart and ditch (A), only possibly included in the first phase of the Castle, were certainly built by 1250. The rampart was at first crowned with a timber palisade, but this was replaced with stonework when the west wall was built. These northern defences were pierced by a gateway with a bridge, probably of timber, over the ditch.

To the west, a stone wall (B) was built about 1270 along the base of the cliff. This linked the northern defences with Castle Vault, and finally enclosed the area of the Outer Bailey. The stone wall (C), possibly the curtain wall of the first phase, still stood, but now only divided the inner and outer baileys. The ditch on

its northern side was filled in, as was the ground behind the new west wall.

The rest of the defences, including the motte and keep, remained fairly unaltered, except for the building of the garderobe tower at the south-western corner of the walls (see p. 20).

# BAILEY NORTH WALL

Very little of what we now see as the North Wall would have been visible just after the wall was completed. The long arcade of stone arches was encased in an earth rampart; they are in fact the foundations of the wall proper. This method of building was used because the arches provided a strong base, while not using as much stone as a solid foundation. This explains the irregularity of some of the arches; they were not meant to be seen, and were built inside pits dug into the rampart.

The wall itself, most of which was demolished long ago, began above these arches. The slight "batter" or inward slope which gave stability to the free-standing wall, can be clearly seen. The change is also marked by the difference between the coursed but rough stone of the foundations, and the ashlar facing of the wall above.

# THE LIME**K**

These building works required a great deal of mortar for the stonework. This was lime mortar, rather than the cement mortar used now, and to keep the builders supplied a large and sophisticated limekiln was built behind the North Wall. Its last firing occurred about 1270, and its capacity for producing large quantities of lime over a long period links it with the building of the North and West Walls.

One particularly puzzling feature encountered during the excavation of the kiln was a large group of skeletons, carelessly buried, which seemed to have lain exposed for some time before burial. They may have been victims of the Black Death, but it is possible that they were victims of a violent episode in Southampton's history – the French Raid.

*Excavations in Madison Street, where the limekiln was discovered. The Bailey North Wall is in the background.*

*The limekiln.*

*Victims of the Black Death, or French raiders? Part of the group of skeletons discovered during excavations of the lime-kiln.*

# THE FRENCH RAID

Although the 1338 raid is always referred to as "The French Raid", and occurred at the beginning of the Hundred Years War, it was hardly an organized attack by a foreign power. The raiders were pirates, probably of several other nationalities as well as Frenchmen, and they were after loot rather than military glory. However, that did not make the raid any less savage.

The raiders sailed up the river and landed on the western quays of the town. There were no city walls to oppose them, and most of the citizens appear to have been in church that Sunday morning. The surprise was so complete that it seems no watch at all was kept on the river approaches, for the ships must have been visible from the town for some time before they landed.

This unpreparedness resulted in the sacking of the town. Archaeologists have found the burnt levels resulting from the firing of houses and shops; documentary evidence records massacre, rape, and the wholesale looting of goods – including the King's wine stocks. If any of the citizens had time to take refuge in the Castle, it is doubtful whether the Castle's defences or garrison were strong enough to protect them: certainly the presence of the Castle did

nothing to protect the rest of the town. The economic effects alone lasted for decades after the raid.

The French Raid may be said to mark the beginning of the end for Southampton Castle. Although its most ambitious phase was yet to come, the Castle had proved unable to defend the town and its people on its own. New defences were needed, and the Castle was relegated to being a second line of defence.

In 1339 – the year following the raid – the King visited Southampton to inspect the defences. He was, undoubtedly, extremely annoyed; having been hurt in his pride by a successful foreign raid and financially by the looting of his goods. The result was that, for the next forty years, all finance and labour was diverted into the completion of the town wall circuit, so that Southampton should be completely enclosed and protected.

Despite the raising of the new town walls, the Castle still had one more phase of usefulness and reconstruction. In 1369 preparations were under way for war with France, and Southampton Castle was judged important in the defences of the south coast. The Castle was garrisoned once more, and in the ten years from 1378 to 1388 a crash rebuilding programme had completely renovated the structure.

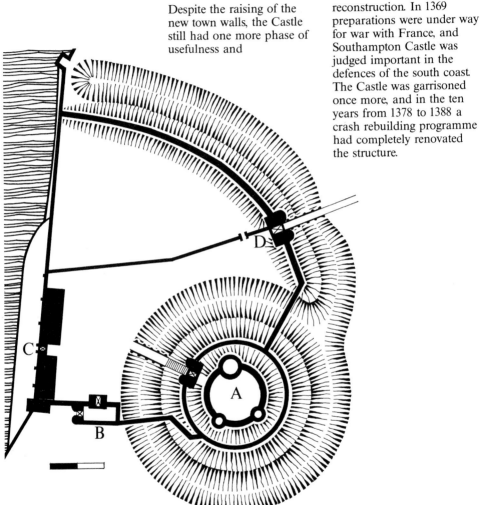

The old shell keep and its decayed buildings were cleared, and a new drum keep with several turrets erected (A). This was surrounded by a curtain wall and the ditch around the motte remodelled in a shallower, more narrow form.

All the gates were improved. New gates on the east and west sides were erected, and the South Gate protected by a barbican (B). The South Gate and wall have long disappeared, but the Watergate in the western wall (C), and the foundations of the East Gate (D), can still be seen.

# CASTLE EAST GATE

The East Gate linked the Castle to the northern part of the town, and was the route by which many of the goods traded at Castle Quay passed in and out of the Castle. It seems narrow for the volume of traffic, but this would have been much easier to defend than a wider entrance. The stone grooves for the portcullis can still be seen; this, together with timber gates, would have blocked the archway that once stood between the two drum-towers. East Gate was excavated, and subsequently restored, in 1960.

# CASTLE WATERGATE

The Castle Watergate protected an important route as it linked the quayside with the interior of the Castle. Although the King had his own warehouses, Castle Hall and Castle Vault, on the quayside itself there were probably other storage buildings inside the Castle. The Watergate was the only route to them for both imports and exports from this quay.

# THE TOWN DEFENCES

But even while this work was under way, other improvements in the defences were making the Castle obsolete. Artillery, although still relatively primitive, was rapidly taking over as the primary weapon for the defences. Gunports were inserted into the West walls of the Castle and town, where they could sweep the approaches to the quays. Thomas Tredyngton was appointed Chaplain to the Castle in 1386; not, apparently, for any saintliness of character but because he was an expert in artillery management. By the time cannon were installed in God's House Tower, the new battery was built in the south-west corner of the town in the early 15th century, Southampton's walls and towers had themselves become a castle – one which could enclose and protect the whole town.

*God's House Tower – the main battery of the town's new defences.*

# ECLINE

From the early 15th century onward the Castle declined, both in its status and structurally. The Crown's interest in the port was diminishing; Southampton's near neighbour, Portsmouth, was beginning its own rise in importance as a major base for the Royal Navy, and probably received far more development funding. The fifteenth century shows steadily increasing structural neglect at Southampton Castle; in 1460 the West Wall is described as "decayed", and in 1498 the North Wall was partly demolished to provide building stone for the Town Watergate Quay.

This trend continued through the 16th century. The Keep seems to have remained fairly intact; Elizabeth I is known to have stayed there in 1569 and 1591, so that it cannot have been too ruinous. But by 1585 most of the Castle perimeter walls had fallen; the Bailey was used by the town's butchers for penning livestock, and by the rest of the townsfolk as a rubbish dump.

In 1618, the Crown finally relinquished its interest in the Castle, and sold the estate for £2,078. This did nothing to halt the decay of the fabric; in fact one of the subsequent owners, Peter Gollop, gave permission for building stone to be extracted from the Castle buildings for use in repairs to the town walls. (In fairness to Mr. Gollop and others, it should be remembered that respect for ancient monuments is a relatively modern concept.

Our ancestors had a very practical outlook: if a wall was standing idle and they wanted the stone for something else, they took it).

The process of demolition and decay continued, almost until the present day. One brighter spot, however, did occur on this gloomy picture. In 1804, the Marquis of Lansdowne decided to built a "castellated mansion" from the remains of the Castle Keep. This kind of aberration was quite common among gentlemen of his time, who combined a hankering after an imagined romantic past with a surplus of money. This was duly built – and demolished, only fourteen years later. Romantic it probably was, but possibly too draughty.

*A View of the Marquis of Lansdownes Castle, Southampton*